Caring For Red Eared Slider Turtles

Facts And Information Regarding To Turtles Caring, Feeding, Habitat, Breeding, Maintenance, Cost, Health, Interaction And Care For Red-Eared Slider Turtles Nests And Eggs

Charlie Furman

Copyright © 2024 Charlie Furman

All rights reserved, no parts and parcel of this book may be reproduced or transmitted in any form or by any means, electronic or mechanical, including photocopying, recording or by any means of information retrieval system, without written permission from the publisher

Table of Contents

- INTRODUCTION 5
- CHAPTER ONE 13
  - PHYSICAL AND BIOLOGICAL TRAITS 13
    - *Red-eared Slider Turtle Growth and Lifespan* 17
- CHAPTER TWO 24
  - ACTIONS AND WAY OF LIFE 24
    - *Environmental and Seasonal Adjustments* 29
- CHAPTER THREE 35
  - HABITAT CONDITIONS 35
- CHAPTER FOUR 41
  - NUTRITION AND DIET 41
    - *Typical Feeding Errors* 46
- CHAPTER FIVE 54
  - WELL-BEING AND HEALTH 54
    - *Illness Symptoms and Preventative Measures* 62
- CHAPTER SIX 69
  - RED-EARED SLIDER TURTLE BREEDING AND REPRODUCTION 69
    - *Care for Red-Eared Slider Turtles Nests and Eggs* 73
- CHAPTER SEVEN 79
  - KEEPING RED-EARED SLIDERS: LEGAL AND ETHICAL ISSUES 79
    - *Conservation Initiatives and Wild Populations: Ethical Issues in Captivity* 83
- CHAPTER EIGHT 87
  - RED-EARED SLIDER TURTLE CARE AND INTERACTION 87
    - *Best Practices for Human-Turtle Interaction* 91

CHAPTER NINE 96

TYPICAL MISCONCEPTIONS AND MYTHS AROUND RED-EARED SLIDERS............................96
  Typical Problems with Red Eared Slider Turtles and How to Fix Them 100

Introduction

Because of their characteristic red markings around their ears, Red Eared Slider Turtles (Trachemys scripta elegans) are among the most popular pet turtles worldwide. Due to the pet trade, these turtles—which are native to the southern United States, especially the Mississippi River basin—have spread to many other regions of the world, where they have occasionally become invasive species.

Physical Characteristics:
Medium-sized turtles with a unique appearance are known as red-eared sliders. Their carapace, or shell, is olive to brown and has yellow patterns and stripes. Their common name comes from their most distinctive characteristic, the red or orange stripe behind each eye. Typically, its plastron—the underside of the shell—has dark, asymmetrical markings and is yellow. While females can develop to a length of 12 inches or more, adult males usually reach about 8 to 10 inches.

Range and Habitat:
Rivers, lakes, ponds, and swamps are just a few of the freshwater habitats that Red Eared Sliders call home in the wild. They favor

places with lots of foliage, places to sunbathe, and still or slowly flowing water. Because of its great adaptability and ability to flourish in a variety of environmental settings, the species has spread outside of its natural area.

Action:
Due to their diurnal nature, red-eared sliders remain active throughout the day. They spend a lot of time in the water and are good swimmers, but they also like to sunbathe on logs, rocks, and other surfaces. Their ability to regulate their body temperature and sustain the growth and functionality of their shells depends on basking. Although they are usually solitary, these turtles sometimes be observed basking in groups in areas that are conducive to their behavior.

Nutrition:
Red-eared sliders are omnivores in the wild. They eat fish, insects, tiny invertebrates, and water vegetation. They continue to need a combination of plant-based and animal-based meals to suit their nutritional demands, even if their diet becomes more plant-based as they become older.

Lifespan and Offspring:

With the right care, red-eared sliders can live for 20 to 30 years in captivity. Their lifespan may be shortened in the wild because of environmental conditions and predation. Usually, mating takes place in the spring and early summer. On land, females dig nests in muddy or sandy soil and lay clutches of 10–30 eggs. After 60 to 90 days of incubation, the eggs hatch, and the young are completely self-sufficient.

The significance of ecosystems

In their natural habitats, red-eared sliders are important. They support the equilibrium of their ecosystems by assisting in the management of aquatic vegetation and insect populations. They may, however, compete with native species for resources in regions where they have been introduced, occasionally leading to ecological imbalances.

Status of Conservation:

Although they are not currently listed as endangered, Red Eared Sliders have faced difficulties in some areas due to their vast dispersion and popularity in the pet trade. While populations are stable in their natural range, they can become problematic in non-native places. Managing these populations and stopping their future spread in non-native habitats are the main goals of conservation initiatives.

In order to properly care for Red Eared Slider Turtles in captivity and manage their influence in non-native environments, it is essential to comprehend their biology and natural history. Because of their resilience and flexibility, these turtles are intriguing subjects for researchers and enthusiasts alike, highlighting the significance of ecological knowledge and appropriate pet management.

Natural Environment

The southern United States, mainly the Mississippi River basin, is home to the Red Eared Slider Turtle (Trachemys scripta elegans). A range of freshwater habitats make up their natural habitat, each of which offers unique circumstances that meet their ecological requirements.

Favorite Settings:
Rivers and Streams: Red-eared sliders prefer areas of rivers and streams that are sluggish or move slowly. In addition to providing plenty of food sources and places to sunbathe, these regions also offer cover from overhanging plants and submerged logs.
Lakes and Ponds: The best habitats are shallow lakes and ponds with an abundance of aquatic vegetation. These habitats offer lots

of places to sunbathe and a variety of prey, including aquatic plants, tiny fish, and insects.

These turtles can also be found in marshes and swamps, where the water is rich in organic matter and frequently warm. Excellent foraging and nesting chances are provided by the muddy bottoms and dense vegetation.

Because of their extreme adaptability, Red Eared Sliders can live in artificial water bodies like urban ponds, agricultural canals, and reservoirs.

Features of the Habitat:

Water Quality: It's important to have fresh, clean water with a moderate temperature. Water temperatures between 75°F and 85°F (24°C and 29°C) are ideal for them. Maintaining water quality requires minimum pollution and appropriate filtering.

Basking Locations: Thermoregulation depends on easily accessible basking locations. Turtles can absorb heat and UVB rays from the sun on logs, rocks, and floating vegetation.

- Vegetation: Water plants offer cover and sustenance. In their habitat, submerged plants like duckweed and elodea are prevalent and provide both food and defense against predators.

Nesting Sites: In order to lay their eggs, female sliders need appropriate terrestrial locations close to bodies of water. The soil at these locations is usually muddy or sandy, making it simple to dig for nests.

The significance of ecosystems

In their environments, red-eared slider turtles contribute to biodiversity and ecological balance in a number of important ways.

1. Trophic Exchanges:
Red Eared Sliders are preyed upon by a variety of species, such as birds, mammals, and larger fish, while they are hatchlings and juveniles. The food web is maintained and their populations are controlled by this pressure from predators.
- Prey: Being omnivores, adult Red Eared Sliders consume a variety of foods. They eat carrion, insects, crabs, tiny fish, algae, and aquatic plants. They contribute to population management, avoiding overgrowth, and preserving ecological balance by eating these species.

2. Cycling of Nutrients:
Detritivores: By frequently consuming dead plant and animal materials, these turtles help aquatic ecosystems break down and recycle organic matter. As a result of their foraging efforts, organic

debris is broken down and nutrients are released back into the water, promoting the growth of aquatic microbes and plants.

3. Control of Vegetation:
Grazers: Red Eared Sliders aid in regulating the growth of aquatic vegetation by consuming it. By preventing some plant species from becoming overly dominant, this grazing promotes diversification and keeps the aquatic plant ecosystem in balance.

4. Seed Spread:
Unintentional Dispersers: Turtles may unintentionally carry seeds through their digestive tracts when they eat fruits and plants. Because these seeds are expelled in diverse places, they help different plant species spread and germinate, which adds to the diversity of habitats.

5. Engineers of ecosystems:
Habitat Modification: Red-eared sliders have the ability to subtly alter their surroundings. Their migrations through foliage can produce tiny clearings and their nesting activities can aerate the soil, changing the habitat structure and encouraging a variety of microhabitats.

Impact of Invasive Species:

Red Eared Sliders have the ability to displace native turtle species in areas where they have been introduced by outcompeting them for resources including food, places to sunbathe, and places to breed. Local ecosystems may be disrupted and native turtle populations may collapse as a result of this competition.

Disease Transmission: New illnesses and parasites that native species are not accustomed to can be brought in by introduced populations, leading to health problems and additional stress on the indigenous fauna.

Because of their roles in trophic interactions, nutrient cycling, vegetation control, and seed dissemination, red-eared slider turtles are essential to the health of their natural ecosystems. Knowing their biological roles and habitat needs emphasizes how crucial it is to preserve their original habitats and control their numbers in non-native places to avoid ecological imbalances.

Chapter One

Physical and biological traits

Red-eared Slider Turtle Anatomy

The unique architecture of Red Eared Slider Turtles (Trachemys scripta elegans) allows them to flourish in both aquatic and terrestrial settings. Here is a thorough examination of their anatomy:

1. The overall structure of the body
The dome-shaped upper shell, called the carapace, shields the animal from predators and environmental dangers. It is made up of keratinous scutes covering bony plates.
Plastron: The lower shell, also known as the plastron, is flat and has protective properties. A bony bridge connects it to the carapace.
Head: The streamlined head has two huge eyes on either side that provide it a broad field of vision. A pointed beak in the mouth is used to rip and bite food.

Red-eared sliders possess four fully formed limbs. The large claws on the front legs are useful for climbing and digging. Swimming is made easier by the stronger, webbed hind legs.

- Tail: Males and females have different sizes of the tail, which is comparatively long. The reproductive organs are located in the longer, thicker tails of males compared to females.

2. The sense organs

- Eyes: Their eyes are designed to see both on land and underwater. Their eyes are protected underwater by a nictitating membrane, often known as the third eyelid.

The tympanic membrane covering the internal ears of Red Eared Sliders aids in their ability to sense sounds and vibrations in the water.

Nose: They can breathe while primarily submerged thanks to the nostrils, which are situated on top of the snout. Their keen sense of smell is essential for locating food.

3. Internal Organs:

- Respiratory System: They can breathe air thanks to their lungs. Despite being mostly aquatic, they need to come up to breathe on a regular basis.

Their heart has three chambers, with two atria and one ventricle, just like that of other reptiles.

The mouth, esophagus, stomach, intestines, and cloaca are all parts of its digestive system. With age, the diet shifts, becoming more herbivorous in adults and more carnivorous in juveniles.

Males have a single penis utilized for internal fertilization, whereas females have paired ovaries and oviducts. Males employ their larger front foot claws for courtship displays.

Structure and Functions of the Shell

One of the Red Eared Slider Turtle's most important and unique characteristics is its shell, which provides protection, structural support, and a way for the turtle to interact with its surroundings.

1. The carapace

Structure: The ribs, vertebrae, and dermal bones are among the roughly 50 bones that make up the carapace. A stiff framework is created when these bones fuse together.

Scutes: Keratinous scutes, which overlap like shingles, cover the carapace. The turtle's age can be inferred from these scutes, which develop in concentric layers as it ages.

The carapace's coloration and patterns aid in concealment among aquatic plants because it is usually olive to brown with yellow markings.

2. Plastron

- Structure: The plastron is covered in scutes and is made up of nine bones. The bony bridge connects it to the carapace.

Function: The plastron supports the internal organs and offers the turtle's underside further protection.

3. The shell's functions include:

Protection: The turtle's shell serves the main purpose of shielding it from environmental dangers and predators. The turtle is protected from attacks by the sturdy structure's ability to withstand considerable force.

One of the functions of the shell is thermoregulation. The turtle's body temperature can be raised by absorbing heat via its shell while it is sitting in the sun. On the other hand, they can move into the shade or water to cool down.

- Buoyancy Control: The turtle can float and swim more effectively thanks to the shell's assistance with buoyancy control. The turtle's stability and balance in the water are aided by the shell's form and weight distribution.

- Sensory Function: The epidermis covering the shell has nerve endings, but the shell itself is not very sensitive. This helps the turtle identify predators or other dangers by enabling it to sense pressure changes and touch.

4. Shell Health:

Shedding: To preserve shell health and promote growth, turtles periodically remove the outermost layer of their scutes.

Diseases and Injuries: In order to prevent major health problems, the shell must be treated as soon as possible for any injuries, infections, or diseases like shell rot.

Red-eared slider turtles have a complex shell structure and anatomy that enable their ability to survive and function in their environments. Every characteristic, from their specialized limbs and sensory organs to their protective carapace and plastron, is essential to their day-to-day existence and long-term survival. Comprehending these traits is crucial for both understanding their ecological responsibilities in the wild and providing appropriate care in captivity.

Red-eared Slider Turtle Growth and Lifespan

Phases of Growth

Throughout their life, Red Eared Slider Turtles (Trachemys scripta elegans) go through several growth stages, each of which is distinguished by certain developmental needs and modifications.

1. Stage of Hatching:
- Size: When hatchlings come out of their eggs, their shells usually measure between 1 and 1.5 inches (2.5 and 4 cm).
Their shell is soft and malleable, and they feature bright, colorful patterning. It is easy to see the crimson stripe behind each eye.
Diet: Hatchlings, which are initially more carnivorous, consume small insects, larvae, and aquatic invertebrates. They need a lot of protein to grow quickly.
Growth Rate: As long as they have access to plenty of food and ideal environmental circumstances, turtles grow quickly throughout this stage, particularly in the first year.

2. Stage of Juvenile:
Juveniles' shell lengths vary from roughly 2 to 4 inches (5 to 10 cm).
- Appearance: Their pigment stays vivid as their shell starts to harden. There may be noticeable dark marks on the plastron.
Diet: They continue to be primarily carnivorous, although they begin eating more plant material.

Growth Rate: In comparison to the hatchling stage, growth starts to decline but stays constant. For their development to be supported, proper diet and habitat are essential.

3. Stage Subadult:

Size: The shell length of subadults ranges from 4 to 6 inches (10 to 15 cm).

- Look: The colors may get a little drab, and the shell gets stronger. Males begin to exhibit sexual dimorphism; their tails and claws grow longer.

Diet: It's crucial to eat a well-balanced diet of plants and protein. They start eating a variety of plant-based and animal-based foods, becoming more omnivorous.

- Growth Rate: Growth is still occurring, but it is happening more slowly. They remain in this stage until they are sexually mature.

4. Stage Adult:

Males are smaller, usually 8 to 10 inches (20 to 25 cm), whereas adult females normally vary from 8 to 12 inches (20 to 30 cm).

- Look: Adults are more subdued in color and have a completely formed, hardened shell. Compared to females, males have thicker tails and longer claws.

Adults still need occasional sources of protein, but their diet is more herbivorous. Their health is supported by a diet high in leafy greens, aquatic plants, and occasionally animal protein.

Growth Rate: After sexual maturity, growth drastically slows down, with sporadic surges influenced by environmental and dietary variables.

Duration of Life

The longevity of red-eared slider turtles is largely dependent on receiving the right care.

1. Out in the Wild:

- Average Lifespan: These turtles usually live between 20 and 30 years in the wild. Disease, food availability, environmental factors, and predation all affect how long they live.

Problems: Predation by birds, animals, and larger fish, habitat degradation, and competition for resources are just a few of the problems that wild turtles must deal with. When compared to individuals kept in captivity, these circumstances may shorten their longevity.

2. In prison:

Average Lifespan: Red Eared Sliders can survive in captivity for 30 to 40 years or longer if given the right care. Some have lived for more than 50 years.

A balanced diet, adequate UVB sunlight, clean water, a well-maintained habitat, and routine health examinations are all crucial components of care. For them to thrive, an appropriate environment that resembles their natural habitat must be provided.

Common Problems: If not given the right care while in captivity, they may develop health problems include metabolic bone disease, respiratory infections, and shell rot. Proper husbandry techniques can help avoid this.

Factors Affecting Lifespan and Growth

1. Nutrition and Diet:

A balanced diet that include both plant and animal products is essential for their development and well-being. Adults need more vegetables, whereas juveniles need more protein.

- Calcium and Vitamin D3: To avoid metabolic bone disease and promote healthy shell and bone formation, a sufficient calcium intake and UVB sun are necessary.

2. Environment and Habitat:

Water Quality: To avoid infections and support general health, clean, filtered water is essential.

Temperature: Healthy digestion and metabolic processes are supported by the right water and sunbathing temperatures. The ideal temperature range for water is 75°F to 85°F (24°C to 29°C), and the ideal temperature range for basking regions is 90°F to 95°F (32°C to 35°C).

Access to a basking area and UVB lighting are essential for calcium absorption and vitamin D3 synthesis, which affects the health of the shell and bones.

3. Medical Care:

Frequent Check-ups: Seeing a reptile veterinarian on a regular basis aids in the early detection and treatment of health problems.

Preventive measures: Maintaining a stress-free environment, keeping an eye out for symptoms of disease, and cleaning the habitat on a regular basis all help animals live longer, healthier lives.

Red Eared Slider Turtle growth and lifespan are affected by a number of factors, such as diet, habitat, and general care. Whether in the wild or in captivity, these turtles can live long, healthy lives if their maturation stages are understood and the right surroundings are provided. Their longevity and general well-being depend heavily on receiving the right care and attention.

Chapter Two

Actions and Way of Life

Everyday Actions and Habits

The variety of daily activities and behaviors exhibited by Red Eared Slider Turtles (Trachemys scripta elegans) reflects their adaptation to both aquatic and terrestrial habitats. Their survival and well-being depend on these actions.

1. Basking
For Red Eared Sliders, basking is an essential pastime. To absorb heat and UVB rays, it entails reclining in the sun on a log, rock, or other surface.
Their body temperature is regulated by basking, which helps them maintain an ideal metabolic rate. Additionally, it facilitates the production of vitamin D3, which is essential for shell health and calcium absorption.
Duration: They may bask for several hours every day, frequently going back to the water to eat or cool off.

2. Swimming

- Principal Activity: The main means of movement and activity is swimming. Red-eared sliders can swim well and move through the water with ease thanks to their webbed feet.

Foraging and Exploration: They swim to forage for food, explore their surroundings, and evade predators. Additionally, swimming gives them exercise, which improves their general health.

3. Feeding and Foraging:

- Diet: Being omnivores, Red Eared Sliders eat a variety of foods, such as carrion, insects, small fish, and aquatic vegetation. As they get older, they eat more plants.

Their feeding behavior involves biting and tearing food with their strong beak. When food is supplied to them in captivity, they might surface because they recognize their caretakers.

4. Taking a break:

Turtles frequently take a nap underwater, usually on the bottom or concealed by aquatic vegetation. When at rest, they are able to hold their breath for long periods of time.

- Terrestrial Rest: After basking, they may occasionally take a nap on land. They may sleep more at night and are less active in the cooler hours of the day.

5. Seasonal Actions:

Brumation: Red Eared Sliders may experience brumation, a dormant state akin to hibernation, in colder climes. They drastically lower their metabolic rate and level of activity at this time, frequently digging burrows in mud or seeking cover underwater.

- Activity Levels: Depending on the season, one may be more active in the warmer months and less active in the cooler ones.

Social Exchanges

Despite being primarily solitary, Red Eared Slider Turtles display a variety of social behaviors. Both in captivity and in the wild, their interactions are visible.

1. The concept of territory

Turtles may vie with one another for the best places to bask. The best spots are frequently occupied by dominant individuals, and inferior turtles may be driven out.

Aggression: Biting and pushing are examples of aggressive actions that can result from territorial disputes. This is especially prevalent in places with limited space or resources.

2. Mating and Courtship:

- Mating Season: Spring and early summer are the usual times for mating. Males become more active during this time and may go looking for ladies.

- Courtship Behavior: When a male swims in front of a female and rapidly vibrates his long claws close to her face, he is engaging in a characteristic behavior known as "fluttering." The female will permit the male to mount and copulate if she is receptive.

Post-Mating: As they look for appropriate nesting locations to deposit their eggs, females may become more solitary after mating.

3. Collective Basking:

Social bathing: Red Eared Sliders are mostly solitary, yet they are frequently observed bathing in groups. Rather than social ties, the availability of basking spots is probably what motivates this activity.

Tolerance: Turtles show tolerance for one another when they are basking in groups. Dominant people may still use force, nonetheless, in order to hold onto their desired position.

4. Interaction:

Visual Signals: Turtles communicate primarily through visual signals. One of the best examples of this is the courting fluttering display.

Chemical Cues: Particularly during the mating season, they may also communicate by using chemical cues. Males can find females with the use of pheromones discharged into the water.

5. Communication with Humans:
- Captivity Behavior: Red Eared Sliders may grow acclimated to being around people in captivity. They might react to feeding times and identify their caregivers.
- Handling: Excessive or inappropriate handling can lead to stress, even though handling is usually tolerated. To reduce tension, it's crucial to handle them sparingly and gently.

The drive to preserve good health, protect resources, and procreate shapes Red Eared Slider Turtles' everyday routines and social relationships. Their actions, which are mostly influenced by their surroundings and the resources that are available, show a balance between solitary and infrequent social encounters. To properly care for them in captivity and recognize their significance in natural ecosystems, it is imperative to comprehend their behaviors.

Environmental and Seasonal Adjustments

The Red Eared Slider Turtle (Trachemys scripta elegans) has evolved a number of adaptations to deal with environmental stressors and seasonal variations. They can survive and procreate in a variety of environments, from warmer temperatures to temperate ones, thanks to these adaptations.

Seasonal Modifications

1. Brumation

Brumation is defined as a condition of dormancy that is comparable to reptilian hibernation. It usually happens in the winter and is a reaction to chilly temperatures.

Behavior: Red Eared Sliders drastically lower their activity levels, metabolism, and food intake when they are brumated. To escape frigid weather, they can burrow into the mud at the bottom of lakes, rivers, or ponds.

Physiological Changes: The turtle's body temperature drops to correspond with its surroundings, and metabolic rates also fall. During this time, they get their energy from stored body fat.

Depending on how severe the winter is, bruising may linger anywhere from a few weeks to several months. Turtles may have shorter or sporadic bouts of brumation in milder regions.

2. Patterns of Seasonal Activity:
Red-eared slider activity increases in the spring and summer as temperatures rise. Growth, reproduction, and nutrition all increase during this time. Turtles are commonly observed basking in order to receive UVB rays and heat, both of which are essential for their physiological and metabolic processes.
Fall: Turtles gradually cut back on their food and activity levels as the weather cools. They may become less frequent baskers and foragers and begin to look for appropriate brumation sites.

3. Adaptations for reproduction:
- Mating Season: Turtles are most active during the spring and early summer, which is when mating usually takes place. In order to attract females, men become more mobile and engage in courtship rituals.
- Nesting: Late spring to early summer is when females lay their eggs. In order to dig nests and lay their eggs, they look for muddy or sandy soil close to bodies of water. The hatchlings emerge during warmer months, which are better for their growth and survival, thanks to the timing of egg laying.

Adaptations to the Environment

1. Thermoregulation

Red-eared sliders are ectothermic, or cold-blooded, which means that they depend on outside heat sources to control their body temperature. By increasing their body temperature, sunbathing aids in immune system, growth, and digestion.

- Aquatic Thermoregulation: Turtles move between various water depths to control their body temperature in addition to basking. While warmer shallow waters aid in raising their body temperature, cooler water offers a haven from extreme heat.

2. Adaptations for respiration:

- Aquatic Respiration: Red Eared Sliders breathe mainly through their lungs, but while submerged, they can also take in some oxygen through their skin and the lining of their cloaca. They can stay underwater for extended periods of time thanks to this adaptability, particularly when brumating or dodging predators.

Turtles frequently come to the surface to breathe. They can breathe while keeping the majority of their body underwater thanks to the nostrils on top of their snout, which reduces their vulnerability to predators.

3. Diet and Feeding:

The omnivorous diet of red-eared sliders enables them to take use of a variety of food sources. This adaptability in diet is essential for survival in a variety of environmental circumstances.

Seasonal Diet Shifts: As they get older and food becomes more or less available, their diet varies. Young animals eat insects, tiny fish, and invertebrates because they are more carnivorous. They eat more plant material as they get older, including algae and aquatic vegetation.

The ability to subsist on stored body fat allows turtles to adapt to times of food scarcity, such as droughts or winter brumation. During brumation, their slow metabolism lessens the requirement for frequent feedings.

4. Use of Habitat:

Diverse Habitats: Due to their high degree of adaptability, Red Eared Sliders may live in a wide range of freshwater environments, such as lakes, ponds, rivers, marshes, and artificial water bodies. They may colonize a variety of habitats because of their adaptability.

Selection of Habitat: They favor areas with a lot of aquatic vegetation, places to sunbathe, and still or slowly flowing water. Thermoregulation depends on basking places, whereas vegetation offers food and shelter.

In response to environmental changes, turtles can travel small distances in search of suitable habitats in the event that drought, pollution, or other factors make their existing home unsuitable. These maneuvers are aided by their superb swimming skills.

5. Avoiding Predators:

Their ability to blend in with their watery environment and evade predators is aided by the hue and patterns of their skin and shells.

Red Eared Sliders can swiftly plunge under the water to burrow into the substrate or conceal themselves among vegetation in reaction to danger. They become less noticeable to predators as a result of this behavior.

Defensive Behavior: They may pull their head and limbs back into their shell to protect themselves when they feel threatened. Many predators can be effectively repelled by the hard shell.

In order to survive in a variety of shifting environments, Red Eared Slider Turtles have evolved a number of seasonal and environmental adaptations. Their exceptional adaptability is demonstrated by their capacity to control their body temperature, modify their nutrition, and take advantage of a variety of settings. It is crucial to comprehend these adaptations in order to conserve them and give them the proper care while they are in captivity.

Their success as a species emphasizes how crucial these tactics are to maintaining their adaptability to environmental shocks.

Chapter Three

Habitat Conditions

Understanding Red Eared Slider Turtles' (Trachemys scripta elegans) natural requirements and trying to replicate them as nearly as possible are key to creating the perfect habitat for these turtles in captivity. This entails setting up the tank appropriately, making sure the water is clean and filtered, and giving enough UVB and basking lights.

The Best Tank Configuration for Captivity

1. Size of Tank:
Minimum Requirements: A tank that holds at least 75 to 100 gallons is necessary for a single adult Red Eared Slider. Although they can start out in smaller tanks, juveniles will soon outgrow them.
A larger tank is always better because it gives you more room to swim and helps keep the water clean. Ten liters of water should be provided for every inch of turtle shell length.

2. Tank Configuration:

Water Depth: The turtle should be able to swim freely in the water. It is advised to go at least twice as deep as the turtle's shell. An mature turtle with a 6-inch shell, for instance, needs water that is at least 12 inches deep.

Land space: In order to fully exit the water, Red Eared Sliders require a dry basking space. It should be simple to get to and spacious enough for the turtle to live happily.

A substrate, such as sand or river boulders, can be put to the tank, however it is not necessary. Steer clear of tiny gravel particles that the turtle might consume. Water quality may be maintained and cleaned more easily with bare-bottom tanks.

3. Accents and Covert Locations:

- Aquatic Plants: Artificial or live plants can serve as hiding places and enrichment. Make sure any live plants can tolerate the turtle's activity and are not harmful.

Commercially available turtle hides, driftwood, and pebbles can all be used to make hiding places and add complexity to the environment, which is good for the turtle's mental stimulation.

Filtration and Water Quality

1. Water Quality:

The water's temperature should be kept between 75°F and 85°F (24°C and 29°C). For constant temperatures, especially in colder locations, use an aquarium heater.

- pH Levels: Red Eared Sliders prefer a pH range of 6.5 to 8.0. To make sure the water remains within this range, test it frequently.

Regular water changes and efficient filtration are necessary to maintain safe levels of ammonia, nitrites, and nitrates. Nitrates should be less than 40 ppm, and ammonia and nitrites should be below 0 ppm.

2. Filtration

Filter Type: Make use of a premium canister filter that is rated for at least twice the tank's volume. Because they are sloppy feeders, red-eared sliders can quickly contaminate waterways with their feces.

Unused food and excrement are among the physical material that is removed from the water by mechanical filtration.

By providing a home for helpful microorganisms, biological filtration converts poisonous nitrites and ammonia into less dangerous nitrates.

Chemical filtering: If mechanical and biological filtering are sufficient, activated carbon can be employed to eliminate odors and discolorations from the water, though it is not usually required.

3. Upkeep:

Water Changes: To preserve water quality, do weekly partial water changes (about 25–30%). Every day, clear away any leftover food and debris.

- Filter Maintenance: Follow the manufacturer's recommendations for cleaning and maintaining the filter. Frequent cleaning guarantees the filter's effective operation.

UVB lighting and basking

1. Area for Basking:

Thermoregulation, digestion, and shell health all depend on basking. For Red Eared Sliders to avoid shell and skin problems, they must thoroughly dry off.

Placement: Make sure the basking area is heated to the proper temperature (around 90°F to 95°F or 32°C to 35°C) by placing it beneath a heat source.

Materials: Use a sturdy platform composed of non-toxic materials, like driftwood, a huge rock, or a basking dock that is sold commercially. Make sure the turtle can easily climb on it and that it is sturdy enough to hold its weight.

2. UVB illumination

The production of vitamin D3, which is essential for calcium absorption and the prevention of metabolic bone disease, depends on UVB sunshine.

Types of UVB Bulbs: Make use of a UVB bulb designed specifically for reptiles, with an output of 5–10% UVB. Compact bulbs and fluorescent tubes are the two primary varieties. Fluorescent tubes are usually more effective and cover a greater area.

The UVB bulb should be positioned around 12 inches (30 cm) above the area where people will be sunbathing. Make sure the turtle and the lightbulb are not separated by any objects that prevent UVB rays, such as glass or plastic.

Lighting Schedule: To replicate natural daylight hours, turn on the UVB and heat lamps for 10 to 12 hours each day to create a day/night cycle.

3. Integrated Lighting Options:

Mercury Vapor Bulbs: These bulbs can be a handy all-in-one option because they emit both heat and UVB light. To prevent overheating, make sure they are positioned at the proper distance as directed by the manufacturer.

Careful consideration of tank size and design, water quality and filtration, and UVB and basking lights are all necessary to provide

Red Eared Slider Turtles with the perfect home. For the health and welfare of these captive turtles, each component is essential. Keepers may make sure their turtles flourish and behave naturally by trying to replicate their natural surroundings as much as possible. For these well-liked pet turtles to have a healthy and engaging environment, regular upkeep and observation are crucial.

Chapter Four

Nutrition and Diet

For Red Eared Slider Turtles (Trachemys scripta elegans) to remain healthy and live a long life, a balanced diet and knowledge of their dietary requirements are crucial. It's critical for their welfare to replicate as much of their natural diet as possible because it can differ greatly from what they eat in captivity.

Natural Food in the Wild

Red-eared sliders are opportunistic omnivores that consume a variety of plant and animal species in their natural environment. As they become older, their diet shifts, with adults consuming more plants and youngsters becoming more carnivorous.

1. Diet for Juveniles:
- Animal Matter: The main source of protein for young Red Eared Sliders' quick growth is animal matter. They eat the following:

Insects and their larvae, such as dragonfly larvae and aquatic beetles

Tadpoles and little fish

Invertebrates that live in water, such as crabs, worms, and snails

"Carrion" refers to deceased animals.

Feeding Behavior: Young animals vigorously search the water for their meal, catching and devouring it with their sharp beak.

2. Adult Nutrition:

- Vegetation: Red Eared Sliders continue to eat some animal products, but as they get older, their diet becomes primarily herbivorous. Typical plant-based diets consist of:

Duckweed, water lilies, water lettuce, and algae are examples of aquatic vegetation.

Fruits and vegetation from the land that fall into the water

Animal Matter: Some foods derived from animals are still consumed by adults, including:

Larvae and insects

Amphibians and little fish

Invertebrates that live in water

Adults use their beaks to bite and rip plants as they search for plant debris near water areas. They also hunt smaller animals opportunistically and scavenge for carrion.

Captive Nutritional Requirements

A balanced diet consisting of both plant-based and animal-based items is necessary to meet the nutritional requirements of Red Eared Sliders kept in captivity. Their development, shell health, and general well-being are all supported by proper diet.

1. Nutrition for Juveniles:
- Protein Requirements: To sustain their fast growth, juvenile turtles require a food rich in protein. Animal products should make up around 70% of their diet.
Commercial Pellets: Premium turtle pellets designed for young turtles offer vital nutrition. They ought to eat these as a mainstay.
- Live and Frozen Foods: To add diversity and enrichment, offer live or frozen insects (such as mealworms and crickets), tiny fish, and invertebrates.
Supplementary Vegetation: To aid in their gradual shift to a more herbivorous diet as they get older, introduce some plant matter to them early on. Provide a little quantity of aquatic plants and leafy greens.

2. Nutrition for Adults:

A balanced diet is necessary for adult Red Eared Sliders, with roughly half of their food coming from plants and the other half from animals.

Commercial Pellets: Adult turtles should regularly consume premium turtle pellets that are designed for them. These pellets are handy and nutritiously balanced.

- Fresh veggies: Provide a range of veggies (carrots, squash, romaine lettuce), leafy greens (kale, dandelion greens), and aquatic plants.

Sources of Protein: Occasionally provide meals derived from animals, such as fish, insects, and invertebrates. In order to prevent excessive protein intake, which might result in health problems, these should be provided less regularly.

To maintain the health of your shell and bones, make sure you are getting enough calcium and vitamin D3. To promote vitamin D3 synthesis, use UVB lighting and cuttlebone or calcium supplements.

3. Feeding Timetable:

Juveniles: To aid in their development, feed juveniles every day. To guarantee a balanced diet, provide a range of foods.

Adults: Give them food three to four times a week or every other day. To avoid overfeeding and problems with water quality, provide enough food that can be eaten in 15 to 20 minutes.

4. Supplements for the diet:

Calcium: To guarantee sufficient calcium intake, sprinkle calcium powder on food on a regular basis. You can also put cuttlebone in the aquarium for the turtle to eat.

Vitamins: To supply vital vitamins and minerals that may be deficient in the diet, take reptile-specific multivitamin supplements as prescribed.

Avoid Over-Supplementation: Take care when taking supplements to prevent hypervitaminosis, which is a dangerous condition caused by an excessive consumption of vitamins.

5. Drinking enough water

Water Availability: Turtles sip water and consume food to stay hydrated. Make sure the tank is continually filled with fresh, clean water.

- Soaking: Give hatchlings and youngsters in particular a small dish of water to soak in. This promotes shedding and helps with hydration.

6. Items to Steer Clear of:

Steer clear of plants that are harmful to turtles, such as avocado, rhubarb, and other decorative plants.

Processed meals, high-fat meats, and dairy items should not be fed to animals because they can cause health problems.

Consuming too many fruits can lead to stomach issues because of their high sugar content.

The health of Red Eared Slider Turtles in captivity depends on feeding them a balanced diet that closely resembles their natural eating patterns. Giving them a range of foods and being aware of their nutritional requirements at different stages of life guarantees that they get the nutrients they need for development, shell health, and general wellbeing. Their health is maintained and nutritional deficits are avoided with the use of suitable supplements, regular dietary monitoring, and dietary modifications. Avoiding toxic foods and staying properly hydrated are two more ways to provide these well-liked pet turtles with the best care possible.

Typical Feeding Errors

For the health and welfare of Red Eared Slider Turtles, appropriate feeding is crucial. A poor quality of life, health problems, and nutritional imbalances can result from a number of typical feeding errors. For proper turtle care, it is essential to comprehend and steer clear of these errors.

1. Overfeeding

Described:
Overfeeding is when turtles are fed more than they require, which frequently results in obesity and other health issues.

Repercussions:
Obesity: Carrying too much weight can strain the turtle's joints and organs, resulting in less mobility and a shortened lifetime.
- Shell Deformities: Pyramiding (raised, pyramid-like scutes on the shell) is one of the shell deformities that can arise from overfeeding, particularly when high-protein diets are consumed.
Bad Water Quality: When too much food breaks down in the tank, ammonia, nitrites, and nitrates rise, which can be dangerous for the turtle and necessitate regular water changes.

Avoidance:
Based on their size and age, give turtles the right amounts of food at the right times. Adults should be fed three to four times a week or every other day, whereas youngsters should be fed every day.
To keep leftover food from contaminating the water, only give the turtle as much as it can eat in 15 to 20 minutes.

2. An Unbalanced Diet

Described:
A diet that is imbalanced and lacks diversity may lead to surpluses or deficits in certain nutrients.

Repercussions:
Vitamin shortages: Insufficient variety can result in shortages in vital vitamins and minerals, including vitamin A, which can cause problems like respiratory disorders, inflamed eyes, and poor shell health.
Overconsumption of animal-based protein can lead to liver illness, renal damage, and shell abnormalities.
Inadequate Calcium: Metabolic bone disease, which is typified by soft, malformed bones and shells, can be brought on by an inadequate calcium intake.

Avoidance:
Offer a well-rounded diet that consists of fresh veggies, aquatic plants, premium commercial pellets, and occasionally animal-based protein.
Make sure the turtle eats both plant-based and animal-based foods, progressively increasing the percentage of vegetable as it gets older.

3. Providing Unsuitable Foods

Described:
Providing turtles with inappropriate diet can result in toxicity, nutritional imbalances, and digestive problems.

Repercussions:
Toxicity: Certain foods and plants, including avocado, rhubarb, and several decorative plants, are harmful to turtles.
Long-term health concerns and digestive disorders might result from eating foods heavy in fat, sugar, or processed substances.
Nutritional Imbalance: Turtles may experience nutritional imbalances and health issues as a result of eating foods not intended for them, such as dog or cat food.

Avoidance:
Investigate and offer suitable diets for turtles, steering clear of known hazardous plants and inappropriate foods.
Adhere to a turtle-specific diet supplemented with safe plants, vegetables, and occasionally protein sources.

4. Insufficient Vitamin D3 and Calcium

Described:
Serious health problems may result from inadequate UVB lighting and calcium for vitamin D3 production.

Repercussions:

Metabolic Bone Disease: This condition is characterized by soft, deformed bones and shells as a result of inadequate calcium and vitamin D3, which weakens the structure and causes discomfort.

Poor Shell Health: Deformities and stunted growth are two symptoms of poor shell health caused by a lack of UVB radiation.

Avoidance:

Add calcium powder to the diet and give cuttlebone to help increase calcium intake.

Make sure the tank has enough UVB light to promote the synthesis of vitamin D3, which is necessary for calcium absorption.

5. Disregarding Personal Nutritional Requirements

Described:

Not taking into account each turtle's unique nutritional needs in light of its age, health, and species-specific needs.

Repercussions:

Malnutrition: While older turtles may consume excessive amounts of protein, which can result in various health problems, younger turtles may not receive enough for growth.

Health Deterioration: Ignoring some medical illnesses that call for dietary changes might make matters worse and make recovery more difficult.

Avoidance:
Adapt the diet to the turtle's stage of life, giving adults more greenery and juveniles more protein.
Keep an eye on health issues and, if necessary, get veterinary advice for particular dietary suggestions.

6. Unreliable Feeding Procedures

Described:
Stress, ill health, and digestive problems can result from irregular food schedules and practices.

Repercussions:
Stress: The turtle's general health and behavior may be impacted by stress brought on by irregular feeding.
Overfeeding or underfeeding can cause digestive issues by interfering with metabolism and digestion.

Avoidance:

A consistent feeding regimen that is suitable for the turtle's size and age should be established.

Keep the kinds and quantities of food provided constant.

7. Not keeping track of and modifying diet

Described:
Nutritional problems may persist if the turtle's health is not regularly monitored and the diet is not modified appropriately.

Repercussions:
Chronic Health Issues: Over time, chronic health problems that are more difficult to address might be brought on by long-term dietary imbalances.

Growth and Development Issues: If a turtle's diet is not modified as necessary, it may not grow properly as a young animal and may cause health issues as an adult.

Avoidance:
Keep a close eye on the turtle's weight, health, and shell condition.

To maintain optimum health, modify the food in accordance with observations and veterinary recommendations.

Red Eared Slider Turtle health and wellbeing depend on avoiding common feeding errors. A balanced diet, avoiding unhealthy foods, getting enough calcium and vitamin D3, and using regular feeding procedures are all crucial parts of good care. A long and healthy life for these well-liked pet turtles is ensured by routine monitoring and modifications based on the turtle's age, health, and particular requirements.

Chapter Five

Well-being and Health

Understanding and preventing common health problems and diseases is essential to ensuring the wellbeing and health of Red Eared Slider Turtles (Trachemys scripta elegans). Maintaining the wellbeing of these turtles depends on identifying the warning signs and symptoms of different illnesses and providing the proper care and treatment.

Common Illnesses and Conditions

1. Infections of the Respiratory System

Described:
Red-eared sliders frequently get respiratory infections, which can be brought on by bacteria, viruses, or fungi. They are frequently brought on by low weather, insufficient sunbathing spaces, or poor water quality.

Signs and symptoms

- Clicking or wheezing noises during breathing

Breathing with an open mouth

The bubbling or discharge from the nose

Inflamed or swollen eyes

Fatigue and appetite loss

Treatment and Prevention:

Preventive measures include keeping the water clean through sufficient filtration, making sure there are many places to bask at the right temperature, and avoiding abrupt temperature changes.

Treatment: For antibiotics or antifungal drugs, consult a veterinarian. Keep the environment as ideal as possible while isolating the afflicted turtle.

2. Rotten Shells

Described:

A bacterial or fungal illness that damages the shell is called shell rot. It frequently happens as a result of accidents, poor water quality, or extended wetness without enough drying time.

Signs and symptoms

Areas of the shell that are soft, discolored, or smell bad

The shell's pitting or peeling

The underlying tissue was exposed.

Areas of the shell that are red or swollen

Treatment and Prevention:

Preventive measures include keeping the water clean, offering a suitable drying place, and making sure the food is well-balanced and contains enough calcium.

Treatment: Use topical antibiotics, keep the turtle dry for long periods of time (dry docking), and clean the afflicted area with antiseptic treatments. For serious situations, see a veterinarian.

3. Bone Metabolic Disease (MBD)

Described:

A calcium or vitamin D3 deficit causes MBD, which results in weak and malformed bones and shells. It frequently results from a poor diet or from not getting enough UVB rays.

Signs and symptoms

Soft or malformed bones and shell

Swollen joints or limbs

Muscle weakness and sluggishness

Having trouble swimming or moving

Treatment and Prevention:

Preventive measures include a healthy diet rich in calcium, cuttlebone or calcium supplements, and adequate UVB lighting to promote the production of vitamin D3.

Treatment: Increase UVB exposure and give calcium supplements. For more thorough treatment, severe cases could need veterinarian involvement.

4. Eye Swelling and Infections

Described:

Vitamin A deficiency, bacterial or fungal infections, and poor water quality can all result in eye infections and edema.

Signs and symptoms

Eyes that are swollen or puffy

Expulsion from the eyes

Eyes that are closed or difficult to open

Inflammation or redness

Treatment and Prevention:

Prevention: Keep the water clean, eat a healthy diet that includes enough vitamin A (such as carrots and leafy greens), and stay away from eye irritants.

Treatment: Rinse the eyes with saline solutions, administer antibiotic ointments as directed, and increase vitamin A intake through food. For severe or ongoing instances, seek veterinarian care.

5. Digestive Problems

Described:
A poor diet, bacterial illnesses, or parasites can all cause digestive issues.

Signs and symptoms
Either loose stools or diarrhea
A lack of bowel movements or constipation
Regurgitation or vomiting
Weight loss and appetite loss

Treatment and Prevention:
Prevention: To lessen bacterial contamination, give a balanced meal, refrain from overfeeding, and make sure the water is clean.
Treatment: For chronic problems or suspected infections, seek veterinary care, hydrate the body, and change the diet to incorporate more fiber (give leafy greens).

6. The parasites

Described:

Turtles may carry external parasites like leeches or ticks, or internal parasites like worms. If untreated, this can lead to a number of health issues.

Signs and symptoms

Parasites that are visible on the skin or in the feces

- Poor development and weight loss

Laziness and a decline in activity

Unusual diarrhea or feces

Treatment and Prevention:

Preventive measures include keeping the area clean, avoiding prey that has been captured in the wild, and placing baby turtles in isolation before reintroducing them to the main habitat.

Treatment: For the proper deworming drugs and extermination of external parasites, seek veterinary care.

7. Deformities of Shells and Pyramiding

Described:

Poor food, overfeeding, or insufficient lighting are frequently the causes of shell deformities like pyramiding, which is characterized by elevated, pyramid-like scutes.

Signs and symptoms
Unusual development of the shell with elevated scutes
The irregular form of the shell
Weak or soft shell regions

Treatment and Prevention:
Prevention: Make sure there is enough UVB light, avoid overfeeding, and give a well-balanced diet with enough calcium.
Treatment: Make dietary and lighting improvements. Long-term dietary and environmental changes may be necessary in severe cases.

8. Deficiency in vitamin A, or hypovitaminosis A

Described:
A lack of vitamin A can cause eye issues, respiratory infections, and general health issues. It is frequently brought on by an imbalanced diet deficient in foods high in vitamin A.

Signs and symptoms

Eyelids and eyes that are swollen

Anxiety related to breathing

Skin that is rough and flaky

Fatigue and appetite loss

Treatment and Prevention:

Prevention: Eat foods high in vitamin A, such as bell peppers, carrots, and dark leafy greens.

Treatment: To guarantee sufficient vitamin A intake, modify the food and give vitamin A supplements under a veterinarian's supervision.

Red Eared Slider Turtles need to be given the right care, eat a balanced diet, and live in a clean environment to stay healthy and happy. Early intervention and treatment are made possible by the ability to recognize the telltale signs and symptoms of common illnesses and health problems. For these well-liked pet turtles to live long and healthy lives, health issues must be avoided and managed with regular veterinary examinations and adherence to best husbandry standards.

Illness Symptoms and Preventative Measures

Important components of responsible Red Eared Slider Turtle (Trachemys scripta elegans) care include monitoring for symptoms of disease and developing a rapport with a reptile veterinarian. Your turtle's health and lifespan can be significantly improved by identifying early symptoms and getting competent veterinary care when necessary.

Indications of Illness

1. Alterations in Eating Patterns and Appetite:
Symptoms include decreased appetite, refusal to eat, or altered feeding habits (e.g., consuming just particular types of food).
Possible Problems: May be a sign of metabolic, dental, or digestive disorders.

2. Weakness and Lethargy:
Symptoms include decreased activity, difficulties swimming, or prolonged periods of inactivity.

Possible Problems: Could indicate underlying medical conditions, metabolic diseases, or infections.

3. Abnormalities of Shells:
Soft patches, discolouration, shell lesions, or shell abnormalities (such pyramiding) are some of the symptoms.
Possible problems include trauma, metabolic bone disease (MBD), calcium insufficiency, and shell rot.

4. Problems with the respiratory system:
Wheezing, open-mouth breathing, nasal bubbles, or difficult breathing are some of the symptoms.
Possible problems include environmental stresses, pneumonia, or respiratory infections.

5. Abnormalities of the nose and eyes:
Symptoms include swollen eyes, nasal or ocular discharge, or trouble opening the eyes.
Possible problems include lung infections, vitamin A insufficiency, or eye infections.

6. Issues with the skin and shell:
Lesions, sores, flaky skin, or unusual shedding are some of the symptoms.

Possible problems include parasites, environmental variables, or bacterial or fungal infections.

7. Modifications in Behavior:
Symptoms include strange behaviors, extensive hiding, or aggression.
Possible problems include stress, alterations in the surroundings, or underlying medical conditions.

8. Gaining or Losing Weight:
Symptoms include weight or body size changes that are noticeable.
Possible problems include parasite infections, metabolic diseases, or nutritional deficits.

9. Insufficient Activity or Excessive Basking:
Symptoms include staying in the water for extended periods of time or excessively sunbathing.
Possible problems include illness, stress, or problems regulating the temperature.

10. Unusual Fecal Production:
Constipation, diarrhea, and odd fecal color or consistency are symptoms.

Possible problems include food imbalances, parasite infections, or digestive disorders.

Care Prevention

1. Frequent Health Examinations:
Make an appointment for routine examinations with a veterinarian who specializes in turtle care. While more frequent visits might be required for young turtles or those with health concerns, annual visits are advised for healthy turtles.

2. Keep an eye on your nutrition and diet:
Give the turtle a well-balanced feed that is suitable for its age and species. Make sure you're getting enough calcium, vitamin D3, and other vital nutrients.
Steer clear of overfeeding and keep an eye on your food consumption to avoid nutritional imbalances and obesity.

3. Preserve Habitat and Clean Water:
To keep the water quality high and avoid bacterial infection, make sure the tank is adequately filtered with clean water.
To promote general health and metabolic function, provide a basking space with appropriate UVB lighting and temperature gradients.

4. Aspects of the Environment:

Keep an eye on and maintain the tank's proper humidity and temperature levels. Steer clear of abrupt changes in the surroundings.

Make use of decorations and substrates that are non-toxic and safe for turtles. Clean and sanitize tank accessories on a regular basis.

5. Observation of Behavior:

Keep an eye out for any changes in your turtle's demeanor, level of activity, or interactions with other turtles in its tank.

Take note of any unusual behaviors or stress-related indicators, as these could point to underlying medical conditions.

6. Preventing Parasites:

To stop the spread of illnesses and parasites, quarantine fresh turtles before reintroducing them to populations that already exist.

Consult a veterinarian for routine fecal examinations in order to quickly identify and treat internal parasites.

Locating and Collaborating with a Veterinarian for Reptiles

For thorough care, locate a licensed reptile veterinarian with expertise in turtles. The following actions will assist you in locating and collaborating with a reptile veterinarian:

1. Investigations and Suggestions:

Consult internet forums, reptile groups, or other turtle caretakers for recommendations.

Examine the experience of nearby veterinarian facilities with reptiles, especially turtles.

2. Knowledge and Expertise:

Select a veterinarian with specialized training and experience in caring for reptiles, such as turtles.

Check their qualifications and ask about their experience with Red Eared Sliders in particular.

3. First Consultation:

Make an appointment for a consultation to talk about your turtle's health, diet, habitat, and any worries you may have.

Assess the veterinarian's attitude toward caring for reptiles and their readiness to respond to your inquiries.

4. Availability of Emergency Care:

Ask about the availability of emergency treatment and after-hours services in case of an emergency.

Understand the clinic's emergency visit and process policies for patients with reptiles.

5. Interaction and Follow-Up:

Communicate openly with your veterinarian about diagnostic procedures, treatment alternatives, and aftercare.

As advised by the veterinarian, keep up with routine examinations to keep an eye on your turtle's health and quickly handle any new problems.

6. Resources for Education:

Consult your veterinarian for informational materials or instructions regarding turtle nutrition, care, and habitat upkeep.

Follow expert guidance to stay up to date on turtle health and wellness best practices.

You may contribute to your Red Eared Slider Turtle's long and healthy life by keeping an eye on its health, giving it the right care and diet, and building a rapport with an experienced reptile doctor. In order to address health issues early and maintain general wellness for these well-known aquatic turtles, prompt veterinary care and preventative measures are essential.

Chapter Six

Red-Eared Slider Turtle Breeding and Reproduction

Red Eared Slider Turtles (Trachemys scripta elegans) engage in unique behaviors and biological processes during breeding and reproduction that are fascinating to see. Turtle keepers can identify and encourage successful breeding in captivity by having a thorough understanding of the turtles' mating habits and reproductive cycle.

Mating Patterns

Seasonal variations and environmental signals influence the unique mating behaviors of Red Eared Slider Turtles. Here is a thorough rundown of how they mate:

1. Seasonal Patterns:

Seasonal variations, especially those related to temperature and daylight duration, have an impact on Red Eared Sliders. In warmer months, they usually become more active, indicating the start of the breeding season.

2. Rituals of Courtship:
Male Display: In order to entice females, males frequently put on ornate displays during courtship. This can involve fluttering their forelimbs to attract attention, head bobbing, and swimming alongside or chasing females.
Female Reaction: By permitting males to approach and mate, females may react favorably to these displays. As a sign of receptivity, they might swim in the direction of the male.

3. Mating
Mounting: The male will mount a female from behind as soon as she demonstrates receptivity. This is a typical activity in which the male uses his large claws on the front limbs to grip onto the female's carapace (shell).
Cloacal Contact: The male's cloaca, which is an opening for the reproductive and excretory systems, aligns with the female's cloaca to transfer sperm during mating.

4. The process of fertilization

Following mating, sperm are transmitted from the male to the female during internal fertilization. Females can fertilize several clutches of eggs from a single mating session because they can retain sperm for several months.

5. Egg Laying and Nesting:

- Nesting Behavior: Following mating, females look for appropriate nesting locations, among other nesting habits. Areas with loose or sandy soil close to bodies of water are usually involved.

- Egg Laying: The female uses her hind limbs to excavate a nest cavity and lays a clutch of eggs after locating a suitable location. Depending on their age, health, and surroundings, Red Eared Sliders can lay anywhere from two to thirty eggs in a clutch.

6. Time Frame for Incubation:

- Natural vs. Captive Incubation: In the wild, eggs are incubated naturally by being buried in the nest. To guarantee ideal conditions and hatch rates, keepers may decide to gather eggs for artificial incubation while the animals are in captivity.

Depending on the temperature and humidity, eggs usually incubate for 60 to 80 days. In general, development happens more quickly at warmer temperatures.

7. Care for Hatchlings:

- Emergence: Using an egg tooth, a temporary structure on the snout, hatchlings break through the eggshell to emerge from the eggs.

- Initial Care: Turtles are self-sufficient and naturally go for water when they hatch. For their first care, create a small, secure space with the right temperature and UVB light.

Factors Affecting the Success of Breeding

Age and Health: Females that are mature (usually between the ages of 5 and 7) have a higher chance of laying fertile eggs. For breeding to be effective, both males and females need to be in good health.

The right amount of humidity, photoperiod (day length), and temperature replicate natural circumstances and encourage breeding activities.

Nutrition: Egg development and reproductive health are supported by a well-balanced diet high in calcium and other nutrients.

Social Compatibility: Verify that men and women get along well and don't treat one another aggressively. To lessen stress during mating and nesting, provide enough room and hiding places.

Red-eared slider turtles engage in intriguing behaviors and biological processes during breeding and reproduction, which are impacted by seasonal variations and environmental cues. Those who wish to breed these well-liked pet turtles in captivity must have a thorough understanding of their mating patterns, nesting habits, and the variables affecting breeding success. Successful reproduction and the wellbeing of adult turtles and their young can be supported by creating ideal environments and paying attention to natural behaviors.

Care for Red-Eared Slider Turtles Nests and Eggs

In the reproductive cycle of Red Eared Slider Turtles (Trachemys scripta elegans), nesting and egg care are crucial phases. It can be easier to successfully mimic these activities in captivity if one is aware of how females nest, lay eggs, and tend to their young in the wild. This is a comprehensive guide to hatchling rearing, egg care, and nesting behavior:

Behavior of Nesting

1. Choosing a Nesting Site:

Female Red Eared Sliders normally select nesting locations close to bodies of water, like lakes, ponds, or marshes, where the soil is adequate, usually sandy or loose.

Provide a nesting location in captivity that is deep enough for the female to excavate a nest cavity and has a substrate mixture of dirt and sand.

2. Digging a nest:

After selecting a good location, the female uses her hind limbs to start excavating a nest cavity. This procedure entails digging a hole that is deep enough—typically 5–10 cm—to hold the clutch of eggs.

3. Laying of Eggs:

The female deposits her eggs into the prepared hole one at a time after excavating the nest cavity. Larger females usually lay more eggs, although Red Eared Sliders can lay anything from two to thirty eggs each clutch.

To reduce vulnerability to predators, eggs are often placed at night or in the early morning.

Egg Maintenance

1. Gathering for Incubation:

To guarantee ideal conditions and hatch rates, many turtle caretakers decide to gather eggs for artificial incubation while the turtle is in captivity. Additionally, it shields eggs from any predators and environmental changes.

To uncover the eggs, carefully excavate the nest cavity, being careful not to damage the eggs' orientation or location too much.

2. Cleaning and Handling:

Be careful when handling eggs; flipping or turning them can upset the position of the embryo and interfere with its development.

Do not wash or clean the eggs unless it is absolutely required. Use a moist towel and lukewarm water to gently wipe an egg that is very filthy.

3. Conditions of Incubation:

Put the eggs in an incubator made especially for reptilian eggs. Red Eared Slider eggs should be incubated at a temperature of approximately 28–30°C (82–86°F).

Keep the humidity level constant (between 80 and 90 percent) to keep the eggs from drying out.

4. Duration of Incubation:

Depending on humidity and temperature, Red Eared Slider eggs usually hatch in 60 to 80 days. In general, development happens more quickly at warmer temperatures.

Regularly check the incubator to make sure everything is steady and make any required adjustments to the parameters.

Growing Offspring

1. The emergence of hatchlings

As soon as the eggs start to hatch, keep a watchful eye on the incubator for any indications that hatchlings are appearing. To crack open the eggshell, hatchlings will utilize their egg teeth, a transient structure on the snout.

2. First Aid:

Move hatchlings to a sanitized shallow water tank that has a ramp or a mild slope so they can easily get water and a place to sunbathe.

Make sure the water is between 24 and 26 degrees Celsius (75 and 78 degrees Fahrenheit) and provide UVB illumination and a heat lamp to create a basking zone with temperatures between 30 and 32 degrees Celsius (86 and 90 degrees Fahrenheit).

3. Nutrition and Feeding:

Provide commercial turtle hatchling pellets or finely chopped leafy greens (like dandelion greens or romaine lettuce) as their major food source.

They occasionally add tiny amounts of protein sources, such as earthworms, bloodworms, or tiny fish, to their diet.

4. Health Care and Monitoring:

Keep a tight eye out for any indications of health concerns in hatchlings, such as deformities in their shells, respiratory troubles, or low appetite.

To avoid bacterial or fungal illnesses, keep the tank clean by changing the water frequently and maintaining ideal water quality.

5. Development and Growth:

In addition to providing suitable hiding places and aquatic plants for enrichment, progressively expand the hatchlings' enclosure as they get bigger.

Keep an eye on their pace of growth and shell development, making sure they get enough calcium and vitamin D3 to support the formation of healthy bones and shells.

Careful attention to detail and adherence to ideal environmental circumstances are necessary for reproducing nesting behavior, egg care, and hatchling raising. Turtle keepers can improve the health and wellbeing of these amazing reptiles in captivity by being aware of the Red Eared Slider Turtles' natural nesting and reproduction activities and by giving them the proper care during incubation and hatchling raising. Supporting hatchlings' growth and maturation into healthy adult turtles requires attentive care, appropriate nourishment, and routine monitoring.

Chapter Seven

Keeping Red-Eared Sliders: Legal and Ethical Issues

Regulations controlling the ownership, trading, and conservation status of Red Eared Slider Turtles (Trachemys scripta elegans) raise a number of ethical and legal issues when keeping them as pets. Comprehending these facets is essential for conscientious ownership and compliance with regulations.

Legal Considerations for Red-Eared Slider Ownership

1. Ownership's legality:
Local Regulations: States, municipalities, and other jurisdictions have different laws pertaining to the ownership of Red Eared Sliders. Researching and comprehending the particular laws in your area is crucial.
Protected Species: Because of their potential to affect regional ecosystems, Red Eared Sliders are regarded as invasive species in

some areas if they are released into the wild. This could limit ownership or necessitate permissions for pet ownership.

2. CITES Rules:

Red Eared Sliders are listed under Appendix II of the Convention on International Trade in Endangered Species of Wild Fauna and Flora (CITES), which governs international trade to prevent unsustainable harvesting for the pet trade from endangering wild populations.

International trade, including the import and export of Red Eared Sliders and their products (such as shells and derivatives), is subject to CITES licenses.

3. Comparing Captive-Bred with Wild-Caught:

Wild-Caught: In order to preserve wild populations, regulations frequently limit the collection and sale of Red Eared Sliders that are captured in the wild. Permits may occasionally be needed for both collection and transportation.

Captive-Bred: Because of worries about disease transmission, the introduction of invasive species, and sustainability, several countries favor or mandate the ownership of pets that are captive-bred.

4. Laws pertaining to animal welfare:

Like all pets, Red Eared Sliders are subject to general animal welfare rules regarding their upkeep. This involves safeguards against abuse or neglect as well as facilities for proper housing, food, and veterinary care.

5. Particular Limitations:

The size and age at which Red Eared Sliders can be lawfully acquired are restricted in several places. Others might need to register or obtain a license in order to keep specific reptile species.

Moral Aspects to Take into Account

1. Conservation Issues:

Originally from some regions of North America, red-eared sliders have spread throughout the world as a result of the pet trade. They are now invasive in some areas, endangering the biodiversity of the area.

Avoiding the release of pet turtles into the wild and aiding in the conservation of native turtle species are examples of ethical considerations.

2. Ownership Responsibilities:

Giving Red Eared Sliders the right attention, habitat, and food throughout their lives is a component of ethical ownership. Understanding their intricate wants and actions is part of this.

3. Awareness and Education:
It's crucial to educate oneself and others on how to properly care for and conserve Red Eared Sliders. Raising awareness of the dangers of introducing non-native species into regional ecosystems is part of this.

4. Encouragement of Sustainable Practices:
Selecting captive-bred Red Eared Sliders from reliable breeders lessens the strain on wild populations and promotes sustainable practices. Be sure to purchase turtles in a morally and legally responsible manner.

Knowing the ethical and legal ramifications of owning Red Eared Slider Turtles includes making sure these creatures receive the right care as pets, adhering to local laws, and fulfilling one's ethical obligations to conservation. Turtle keepers may improve the welfare of Red Eared Sliders and their natural habitats by supporting conservation initiatives, encouraging appropriate ownership practices, and remaining up to date on pertinent regulations. To guarantee compliance and moral care of these well-liked pet turtles, always check with local authorities or reptile experts for specific rules and regulations in your area.

Conservation Initiatives and Wild Populations: Ethical Issues in Captivity

Red Eared Slider Turtle (Trachemys scripta elegans) captive ethics cover a variety of issues pertaining to conservation initiatives and their effects on natural populations. Comprehending these concerns is essential for responsible pet ownership and making a constructive contribution to this species' conservation.

Conservation Situation and Difficulties

1. Native Distribution and Habitat:
Native to the southeast region of the United States, red-eared sliders mostly live in freshwater environments like lakes, ponds, and slowly flowing rivers.

The introduction and settlement of these animals in Europe, Asia, and portions of Africa can be attributed to human activity, habitat destruction, and the pet trade.

2. Concerns about Invasive Species:
As invasive species, Red Eared Sliders can be extremely dangerous in places where they have been introduced outside of their natural habitat.
These turtles have the ability to change ecological dynamics, outcompete native species for resources, and possibly infect other wildlife populations with diseases.

3. Challenges in Conservation:
Because of habitat degradation, pollution, climate change, and direct exploitation for the pet trade, native turtle conservation efforts frequently encounter obstacles.
Conservation groups study wild populations, preserve native habitats, and put plans in place to lessen the effects of invasive species like Red Eared Sliders.

Ethics in Captivity: A Consideration

1. Conscientious Ownership:

The conservation status of Red Eared Sliders and possible effects on wild populations should be taken into account while deciding whether to retain them in captivity.

Proper care, appropriate housing, and nourishment are all part of responsible ownership, as is reducing the possibility of escape or release into the wild.

2. Steer clear of release into the wild:

Local ecosystems are seriously endangered when pet turtles, particularly non-native species or those from other geographic areas, are released into the wild.

Released turtles have the potential to upset ecological equilibrium, spread illnesses, and compete with native animals for resources.

3. Encouragement of Conservation Efforts:

By raising awareness of the effects of invasive species and taking part in initiatives to save native turtle habitats, pet owners and enthusiasts can aid conservation efforts.

The demand for turtles taken from the wild is decreased by supporting respectable breeders who place a high value on ethical and sustainable breeding methods.

4. Outreach Education:

Responsible stewardship is promoted by educating oneself and others on the Red Eared Sliders' natural history, behavior, and conservation requirements.

The wellbeing of captive turtles is guaranteed, and adverse effects on wild populations are reduced, by promoting ethical pet ownership practices, such as appropriate enclosure design, nutrition, and medical attention.

Red-eared slider turtle ethics in captivity place a strong emphasis on the value of conservation knowledge, conscientious ownership, and backing for programs that preserve natural wildlife habitats. Turtle keepers can make a big difference in protecting biodiversity and encouraging sustainable pet trade practices by being aware of the ecological effects of invasive species and actively supporting conservation initiatives. To maintain a positive relationship between pet ownership and environmental conservation, always put the welfare of both captive and wild turtles first.

Chapter Eight

Red-Eared Slider Turtle Care and Interaction

Care must be taken when handling and engaging with Red Eared Slider Turtles (Trachemys scripta elegans) in order to minimize stress and guarantee the turtle's safety and wellbeing. This is a thorough reference to safe handling methods and stress-reduction tactics for these well-liked aquatic pets:

Techniques for Safe Handling

1. Method and Readiness:
Wash your hands well with soap and water before handling your Red Eared Slider to get rid of any impurities or smells that could annoy the turtle.
To avoid frightening or upsetting the turtle, approach it carefully and don't move quickly.

2. Supporting and Lifting:

Using both hands, softly but firmly grasp the turtle. To uniformly distribute the turtle's weight, support its body, especially its middle and hind limbs.

To prevent damage to the turtle's spine or shell, do not lift it by its shell alone.

3. Managing Posture:

To reduce the chance of falling, hold the turtle close to your body and maintain it at or close to ground level.

Make sure your hands are firmly in place to stop the turtle from wriggling or escaping your hold.

4. Orientation of Shell:

The turtle should be handled with its shell facing up. By doing this, excessive pressure on the plastron (bottom portion of the shell) is avoided and the shell's natural curvature is preserved.

5. Preventing Overuse of Force:

The turtle's body or limbs should never be squeezed or subjected to extreme pressure. Due to their sensitivity to pressure, turtles may become agitated or hurt if treated aggressively.

6. Reduce the Handling Time:

To prevent causing the turtle undue stress, keep handling sessions brief (ten to fifteen minutes).

After handling, quickly return the turtle to its enclosure so it can recuperate in its comfortable surroundings.

Reducing the Turtle's Stress

1. Establish a Safe Environment:

To increase the turtle's sense of security, construct the enclosure with lots of hiding places, locations for sunbathing, and clean water.

To reduce health problems linked to stress, maintain consistent environmental conditions, such as the right temperature and water quality.

2. Regularity and Forecasting:

To make the turtle feel safe and comfortable with human contact, establish a regular feeding, cleaning, and handling schedule.

To lessen stress, minimize abrupt alterations or disturbances in the turtle's surroundings.

3. Communication and Observation:

While touching the turtle, pay attention to its behavior and body language. Rapid movements, hissing noises, or attempts to retreat within its shell are all indications of stress.

Keep your voice down and refrain from making loud noises or sudden movements that can scare the turtle.

4. Observe personal space:

If the turtle exhibits any symptoms of discomfort or stress while being handled, let it hide or retreat. Avoid invasive or protracted interactions and respect its demand for privacy.

5. Encouragement in a positive way:

Positive experiences, such giving the shell a reward or soft stroking, should be linked to handling sessions. This lessens hesitation or fear in subsequent encounters and fosters trust.

The safety, comfort, and wellbeing of Red Eared Slider Turtles should come first while handling and engaging with them. You may maintain the health and happiness of your pet in captivity while cultivating a good relationship with it by using safe handling practices, reducing stress, and honoring the turtle's natural habits. To guarantee happy and stress-free interactions for you and your turtle friend, always put the turtle's needs first and create a nurturing environment.

Best Practices for Human-Turtle Interaction

Various facets of handling, caring for, and interacting with Red Eared Slider Turtles (Trachemys scripta elegans) are included in human-turtle interaction. Understanding the turtles' needs and habits as well as putting best practices into practice to support their wellbeing are necessary to make sure these interactions are constructive and advantageous for the turtles. A comprehensive guide to human-turtle interaction best practices may be found here:

1. Comprehending Turtle Behavior

1. Red Eared Slider Turtles are renowned for their semi-aquatic lifestyle, which includes spending a considerable amount of time in the water and relaxing on land. They may act in ways like withdrawing inside their shells when under stress or feeling threatened, and they are normally cautious around people.

2. Individual Variability: Turtles may have unique inclinations and personalities. While some might be more reserved or easily agitated, others might be more accepting of handling and

interaction. Fostering a great engagement experience with your turtle requires an understanding of its distinct behaviors and preferences.

2. Techniques for Safe Handling

1. Preparation: Before handling the turtle, properly wash your hands to get rid of any smells or impurities that could startle it. Be cool when approaching the turtle and refrain from making abrupt movements.

2. Supportive Handling: To prevent straining the turtle's limbs or shell, lift it with both hands while evenly supporting its body. The turtle may get hurt if you lift it by its shell alone.

3. Shell Position: To preserve the turtle's natural posture and lessen strain on its shell, hold it with its shell facing up.

4. Minimal Handling Time: Because extended handling might stress the turtle, keep handling sessions brief (10–15 minutes). After handling, quickly return the turtle to its enclosure so it can relax without being disturbed.

3. Establishing a Positive Atmosphere

1. Enclosure Design: Create a roomy, well-equipped habitat with enough swimming room, tanning spots, and hiding places. Use appropriate substrates, plants, and decorations to replicate natural settings.

2. Maintain a stable habitat by keeping the lighting, water temperature, and water quality constant. Turtles may experience stress and health problems as a result of changes in these variables.

3. Predictability and Routine: Create a consistent schedule for contact, cleaning, and feeding. Turtles might get anxious by abrupt changes or disturbances and prefer consistency.

4. Reducing Stress

1. Communication and Observation: Pay attention to your turtle's reactions and body language when you are interacting with it. It may move quickly, hiss, or try to hide inside its shell as a sign of stress. React coolly and modify the conversation as necessary.

2. Respect Personal Space: If the turtle exhibits symptoms of stress or discomfort, let it hide or withdraw. Respect its right to privacy and refrain from pressuring them to interact.

3. Positive Reinforcement: Link interactions to rewarding experiences, such giving hugs or food. This promotes confidence and trust in interpersonal relationships.

5. Well-being and Health

1. Nutrition: Give Red Eared Sliders a well-balanced diet that includes leafy greens, commercial turtle pellets, and sporadic protein sources. Make sure you are taking enough vitamins and calcium supplements.

2. Veterinary Care: Make an appointment for routine examinations with a reptile veterinarian who specializes in caring for turtles. To preserve good health and avoid illnesses, take quick care of any health issues.

6. Possibilities for Education

1. Learning and Awareness: Inform yourself and others about the Red Eared Slider Turtle's natural history, current state of conservation, and maintenance needs. Encourage conservation initiatives and responsible pet ownership.

2. Public Engagement: Take part in outreach initiatives or educational programs to increase public knowledge about turtles and their environments. Promote responsible wildlife encounters and conservation measures.

The comfort and well-being of Red Eared Slider Turtles should come first in human-turtle interactions, and both the turtles and their caregivers should have a good time. Turtle lovers may assist the welfare and conservation of these amazing aquatic reptiles by learning about their behaviors, using safe handling practices, fostering a caring environment, and raising awareness through education. Always approach relationships with respect, patience, and a dedication to giving your turtle partner the best care possible.

Chapter Nine

Typical misconceptions and myths around red-eared sliders

Compared to other reptiles, Red Eared Slider Turtles (Trachemys scripta elegans) require less maintenance and have a unique appearance, making them attractive pets. But there are a number of myths and false beliefs about these turtles that can cause people to misunderstand how they should be cared for, how they behave, and what they need in general. A thorough examination of several widespread misconceptions regarding Red Eared Sliders may be found here:

Myth 1: Red-eared Sliders Don't Get Big and Take Up Much Room

Reality: The idea that Red Eared Sliders are little and don't need a lot of room is one of the most persistent misconceptions about them. In actuality, these turtles can become rather huge over time, with shells up to 12 inches (30 cm) or longer. A large enclosure with enough swimming space, tanning spots, and mobility is necessary for the proper care of adult Red Eared Sliders.

Myth 2: You Can Keep Red-Eared Sliders in a Tiny Tank or Bowl

The truth is that Red Eared Sliders cannot survive in little bowls or tanks, despite what many people think. Being energetic swimmers, these turtles require a sizable water habitat in order to exercise, display their natural habits, and stay healthy. A tank or pond that can accommodate at least 40 gallons of water per turtle, along with extra room for basking areas, is usually part of a suitable setup for adult Red Eared Sliders.

Myth 3: UVB Lighting Is Not Necessary for Red-Eared Sliders

Reality: The health and welfare of Red Eared Sliders depend on UVB lighting. These turtles' metabolism of calcium, which is essential for strong bones and shells, is aided by UVB sunshine. Red Eared Sliders are susceptible to metabolic bone disease (MBD), a dangerous ailment that can impair their general health and lifespan, if they do not receive enough UVB radiation.

Myth 4: Heat Lamps Are Not Necessary for Red-Eared Sliders

As ectothermic reptiles, red-eared sliders depend on outside heat sources to maintain a consistent body temperature. To provide a warm basking area where turtles may efficiently thermoregulate and digest their food, a heat lamp or basking light is necessary. For the basking region to support their metabolic processes, the temperature should be between 85 and 90°F (29 and 32°C).

Myth 5: Low Maintenance Pets Are Red-Eared Sliders

Reality: Red-eared sliders are not low-maintenance pets, despite their relative adaptability and hardiness. Maintaining water quality, giving them a variety and balanced feed, making sure they have enough UVB and heat sources, and often checking on their health are all necessary for proper care. Long-term dedication to their care is crucial because they can survive in captivity for several decades.

Myth 6: Children Make Good Pets with Red-Eared Sliders

Reality: Although they can make interesting pets, small children may not be able to handle red-eared sliders without adult supervision and engagement. Youngsters need to comprehend the responsibilities of keeping a pet turtle, which include handling them carefully, maintaining good cleanliness, and honoring their desire for privacy and quiet.

Myth 7: Goldfish Can Help Red-Eared Sliders Succeed

The truth is that Red Eared Sliders are opportunistic feeders and may consume small fish in the wild, but a captive turtle's diet that consists only of feeder fish or goldfish is not nutritionally balanced. These fish may have thiaminase, an enzyme that can obstruct the absorption of vitamin B, and are frequently lacking in vital minerals like calcium. Commercial turtle pellets, leafy greens, vegetables, and sporadic protein sources such cooked meats or insects should all be a part of a Red Eared Slider's diet.

Myth 8: Filtration Is Not Necessary for Red-Eared Sliders

Reality: Keeping the water of a Red Eared Slider's tank clean and healthy requires proper filtration. If not adequately filtered, the excrement produced by these turtles can rapidly deteriorate the quality of the water. It is advised to use a mix of chemical, biological, and mechanical filtration to keep the water parameters at ideal levels for the turtles' health and to get rid of trash and dangerous pollutants.

It's critical to dispel common misconceptions about Red Eared Sliders in order to guarantee their welfare and appropriate treatment while in captivity. Turtle keepers may create a habitat that supports the natural habits of these turtles and fosters long-term health by knowing their genuine needs, which include room, food, lighting, and filtration. Any questions can be answered and Red Eared Sliders can be given the finest care possible for the rest of their lives by speaking with reliable sources and knowledgeable reptile doctors.

Typical Problems with Red Eared Slider Turtles and How to Fix Them

Identifying and resolving a range of concerns that may emerge in the care and surroundings of Red Eared Slider Turtles is part of troubleshooting frequent problems with these turtles. To maintain the health and wellbeing of your Red Eared Slider, follow our comprehensive information on troubleshooting and fixing common issues:

1. Problems with Water Quality

Problem: Red-eared sliders may suffer from respiratory infections, skin disorders, and shell rot as a result of poor water quality.

Steps for Troubleshooting:
Verify Filtration: Make sure the size of your turtle's enclosure matches the capacity of your filtration system. To efficiently remove waste and preserve water clarity, take into account a combination of chemical, biological, and mechanical filtration.
- Track Nitrite and Ammonia Levels: Use a dependable test kit to test water parameters on a regular basis. Nitrite and ammonia levels should be 0 parts per million (ppm). Elevated levels suggest overfeeding or insufficient filtering.
Do Regular Water Changes: To eliminate accumulated waste and preserve water quality, change 25–50% of the water every week or as needed. To remove chlorine and chloramines from tap water, use a dechlorinator.

2. Problems with Shell Health

Problem: Environmental stressors, insufficient UVB exposure, or poor diet can all lead to shell issues like fragile shells, shell rot, or shell lesions.

Steps for Troubleshooting:

Assure Proper Diet: Offer a well-rounded diet consisting of vegetables, leafy greens, commercial turtle pellets, and sporadic protein sources. Supplementing with calcium and vitamin D3 is essential for shell health.

- UVB Exposure: To help your turtle metabolize calcium and preserve shell strength, make sure it gets 10–12 hours of UVB light per day. For maximum efficacy, place UVB lamps as directed by the manufacturer.

Keep an eye on the basking temperature: To aid with digestion and thermoregulation, keep the basking region between 85 and 90°F (29 and 32°C). Shell health may be impacted by inadequate basking heat.

3. Problems with the Respiratory System

Problem: Inadequate basking temperatures, bad water quality, or drafts in the turtle's surroundings can all lead to respiratory illnesses.

Steps for Troubleshooting:
Verify the basking conditions: Make sure there is a suitable temperature gradient and that the region is warm and dry. For efficient body temperature regulation, turtles require a warm basking area.

Assess Water Quality: Respiratory problems may result from poor water quality. With appropriate filtration and frequent water changes, you can keep your water pure.

Speak with a Veterinarian: See a reptile veterinarian right once for diagnosis and treatment if your turtle is displaying signs like wheezing, nasal bubbles, or lethargy.

4. Deficiencies in Nutrition

Problem: Vitamin (such A and D3) and mineral (like calcium) deficits brought on by inadequate nutrition might impair immune system function and general health.

Steps for Troubleshooting:

Offer a Diverse Diet: Provide a range of foods such as commercial turtle pellets, vegetables (carrots, squash), dark leafy greens (kale, collard greens), and occasionally fruits or protein sources (insects, prepared lean meats).

Supplementation: As advised by a veterinarian, make sure calcium and vitamin D3 supplements are given. Steer clear of excessive supplementing as this may result in health issues.

Keep an Eye on Feeding Habits: Make sure your turtle is eating a balanced diet by keeping an eye on how it feeds. Adapt offerings to dietary requirements and inclinations.

5. Modifications in Behavior

Problem: Behavior changes like reduced activity, sluggishness, or hostility may be signs of underlying medical conditions, stress, or environmental influences.

Steps for Troubleshooting:
Examine the Turtle's Environment: Look for any stressors in the turtle's enclosure, such as insufficient hiding places, loud noises, or excessive handling.
Verify the environmental conditions, including the water quality, UVB exposure, and temperature. Turtles may become stressed by alterations or disturbances in their surroundings.
Seek Veterinary Advice: A reptile veterinarian should be consulted if there are persistent or worrisome behavioral changes. They are able to identify medical conditions and suggest the best course of action.

6. Trauma or Injury

Problem: Shell damage or wounds may result from falls, rough handling, or hostility from tank mates.

Steps for Troubleshooting:

Safe Handling: To avoid falls or injuries, handle your turtle gently at all times and support its body. Don't lift just by the shell.

Keep an eye on Tank Mates: If you have several turtles or other tank mates, make sure they get along and keep an eye out for any aggressive behavior. Give people enough room and places to hide.

Treat Injuries Right Away: Clean and tend to any wounds or damage to the shell as soon as possible. For advice on how to treat wounds properly and avoid infections, speak with a veterinarian.

7. Stressors in the Environment

Problem: A turtle's health and behavior might be affected by environmental stressors including loud noises, abrupt movements, or insufficient hiding places.

Steps for Troubleshooting:

Provide a Secure Environment: Establish a serene and safe environment with enough places to hide, sunbathe, and create visible barriers.

Reduce Disturbances: Steer clear of loud noises or abrupt movements close to the turtle's enclosure. Minimize stressors that could interfere with the turtle's sleep or routine.

Observe Behavior: Keep an eye out for indications of stress in your turtle's behavior, such as excessive hiding or refusal to eat. Take care of any stress-causing environmental conditions.

General Troubleshooting Advice:

Frequent Monitoring: Keep track of the temperature, water quality, and the behavior and well-being of your turtle on a regular basis.

Consult Reputable Sources: To learn about frequent problems and remedies, consult trustworthy sources such veterinary manuals, trustworthy websites, or books on turtle care.

Seek Veterinary Care: Consult a qualified veterinarian with experience in caring for reptiles if issues continue or get worse after troubleshooting attempts.

You can guarantee a healthy and flourishing habitat for your Red Eared Slider Turtle by quickly recognizing and resolving frequent problems. Their general health and longevity in captivity are influenced by proactive habitat management, appropriate care procedures, and routine observation.

Made in the USA
Coppell, TX
09 February 2025

45590189R00059